Theatrix:
Poetry Plays

OTHER BOOKS BY TERESE SVOBODA

POETRY
Professor Harriman's Steam Air-Ship
When the Next Big War Blows Down the Valley:
Selected and New Poems
Weapons Grade
Treason
Mere Mortals
Laughing Africa
All Aberration

FICTION
Great American Desert
Bohemian Girl
Pirate Talk or Mermalade
Tin God
Trailer Girl and Other Stories
A Drink Called Paradise
Cannibal

BIOGRAPHY
Anything That Burns You: A Portrait of Lola Ridge, Radical Poet

MEMOIR
Black Glasses Like Clark Kent

TRANSLATION
Cleaned The Crocodile's Teeth

For
George McWhirter
who wrote
the line is a stage.

CONTENTS

An Introduction in the Style of an Introduction

When I was a little boy, which I still am and I'm also a grown-up, on rainy days I would stage plays for the benefit of my sanity. In my living room, the chair would be a deserted island, the coffee table a boiling sea of suck-fire, the curtains merely sheers, the window over there a giant's droopy and gooey eyeball, two dogs my companions, renamed Nip and Tuck for the journey, and the ceiling fan the swirling swords of the Almighty Monster, His Holiness, Holy Cannoli.

I would externalize. I would imagine. I would propagate my universe, and propagandize on behalf of the imagination, and my authorial and piratical inclinations.

I would be a boy, a girl, a man, a woman, all. My selves and I would *act*.

Terese Svoboda's astonishing new work, *Theatrix: Poetry Plays*, is a little like this, only a lot more. And because today's a rainy day in a terrible season of human terribleness – the downpour's torrential, *it's raining awful out there*, as we say in this region of The Introduction – Svoboda's marvelous book of curious fancies and fancy curiosities and sad delights and delightful sadnesses is not just necessary, it's required.

Take Shakespeare. Read him a lot, know more than before. Then take a relentless interest in the behavioral weirdness of the line of poetry, which Svoboda the poet has, and a dialogical/diabolical understanding of consciousness as character, which Svoboda the novelist has, and an eccentric and flamboyant comprehension of form, which Svoboda the Svoboda has. Next give us voices, and their own inner voices, the ways we have made gender our playmates, and how we make our bodies the play. Then stand close, and watch the players play.

Style is a form of feeling, of course. Feeling is also a form of style. Svoboda knows these knowings as well as any writer going. And wow, check out the lapidary, the aviary, the hatchery, the haberdashery, and the caravansary of her jingling lingo; and zow, look what her poetry plays do when the words are banged together thus, cymbalically. Holy Cannoli, indeed.

I love this brilliant book. You will too.

– *Alan Michael Parker*

ACKNOWLEDGMENTS

Many thanks to the editors of the following periodicals where these poems first appeared:

Bat City: "Blank Pink Mall"

Denver Quarterly: "Dark Daddy"

Interim: "Spectacle" and "Chair Theater"

Lana Turner Journal: "Scatter Force Two," "[to our ears]," and "A Tripod Provides Stability Against Downward and Horizontal Forces"

Litmag: "Verona Not Venice"

Mad Hatter's Review: "The Glassine [a very thin and smooth paper which is air and water resistant]"

Plume: "The Comedienne"

Poetry: "Shame Helps"

Poetry Spotlight: Best American: "Out Of Ringing Ears" and "*What?* Is Your Line"

Southampton Review: "King Leer"

Swwim: "Silverware Dialogue"

With enormous gratitude to Headlands Center for the Arts, Virginia Center for the Arts, Swan Island Lighthouse Keeper's House Residency, Yaddo, James Merrill House, Rowland Writers Retreat, and Hawthornden Castle where thoughts were thought and paper blackened. Lest you think I ever forget: Steve Bull of course, Alan Michael Parker, Stephanie Strickland, Kristine Snodgrass and Lynne Knight at Anhinga, and Kristina Marie Darling, a darling.

Theatrix:
Poetry Plays

Wrongness, ceremony and a bit of demonism.
— Mac Wellman

What are you knotting there, my man?
The knot.
— Melville's *Benito Cereno*

CAST
(IN ORDER OF APPEARANCE)

Stage Manager
Set
Marching Soldiers
Comedian Jack Benny
Dramaturg
Me
WE
Third Lover
First Lover
Second Lover
Emma's Corpse
Fourth Lover
Poe
Debussy
Not to Mention
(Ben) First Actor
(Beatrice) Second Actor

Many non-speaking parts, or parts that can't speak, or parts speaking inaudibly.

ONE

Stage Manager: *Lights Up*

[Giant hand moves the parade ground stage left.]

SET: *OMG, the alien blows through the one window not yet painted over.* [dot, dot, dot.]

Dancers tambourine [in shivers] in front of the guns.

What about this is false: the scale, the alien plastered to the wall in a green you can't see? the trust you place [like an acorn] in the seat?

MARCHING SOLDIERS: *Drape the pretty flowers on the muzzle.* [Whereupon the put upon i.e. ladies, leap like petals falling off, each a drop of solder for the soldiers, their feet lead.]

Who me? to the elderly mirror.

[The play?] "Hair."
COMEDIAN JACK BENNY: *Did you happen to notice if any of them were Jewish?*

The alien drops its eyes to the [credits on] paper.

DRAMATURG: *Not only did many of the lyrics in the play not rhyme, but many of the songs didn't really have endings, just a slowing down and stopping, so the audience didn't know when to applaud.*

ME: *Beckett-it.*

HBO'S Chernobyl

I want this to scare you [your eyes so delicately aspic, watching].
Only one on the bridge lives.

The dog cringes from the resignation floating grayly down.
[Which rhymes with nation]. Self-interest, a flood of it.

The curtains keep fluttering.

If the rhino [not the elephant] stalwart in the absurdist room
packed with isotopes guarded by men full of flesh and blood

withholds catharsis, so be it. Laugh, but someone
has to wonder, someone with the iambs to put out flames

or the leisure [no, the terror] to compose the bridge

thirty years later. The spectators do not yell
as if a war [or even a holiday] beckoned.

That cat on the couch? The bird twitchy on the pavement
after the school-bound kids chase off-screen?

No animal was injured in the making of the media,

and no farmer refused to harvest Ukraine's wheat.
Knowledge was eaten, [a plume of it]

and all the rain there is cannot quench the truth,

nor evacuate it. Man imagines this [and this
comes about]. The brain folds – ask the media.

SANDWICH

Across the stage of the plains interstate inter state dell and dell and plains, there is a scene where they run out of gas.

You – in the white shirt –

I'm just as scenic. Listen: *There was a tremendous knocking.*

Knock, knock.
No joke.

They put him in a closet.
Not a dell?

They put him in a closet and the door, hung wrong, had a gap at the bottom where you could shove a whole sandwich through, though the bread got a little dirty. As for thirst, I don't know. No light of course except through the gap so the sandwich came in dark and dirty.

Whispering voices from the phone.

Can you get it?

There was a tremendous knocking across the plains, sometimes as if on a windowpane. Sometimes enough to break it, or else from below.

You don't know that.

It's a kind of knowing, just like the knocking you say you heard just after they ran out of gas. And who is the they anyway? The usual suspects, M and F, old while you're not and because of that, always running out of gas.

They wished there were windows. There were sandwiches they made for themselves, they didn't shove them all.

The door will be open. But that means mud will be tracked in by the gas-less, earning alienation.

Time gaps while they run away like that, after someone finds him in the closet. Maybe the someone went looking for a coat, a winter coat that he thought he had hung in there. Pee-You.

M and F forgot their homemade sandwiches and they ran out of gas.

How do you know?

Someone called. Someone said, Look in the closet.

It was you.

I was wearing a white shirt, easy to spot. I didn't need a coat.

They walked a long way before anyone picked them up, and it never stopped raining. The dell came up while they were walking.

A farmer in the dell. A big Ford truck with 4WD.

Interstate.

No trace of footsteps because of the rain.

Interstate gets into the car like a hum. You would think they were fleeing the site but no, they just ran out of gas.

What if guilt is free like the falling of rain instead of cooped up in a closet? He was crying.

I'm not related. I'm not the last or the late. I'm not – really.

I say: there was a scene and someone went inside but whether –

A white shirt is easy enough to spot. Dirt just falls on it.

There was a tremendous knocking.

A Tripod Provides Stability Against Downward and Horizontal Forces

> By the pricking of my thumbs,
> Something wicked this way comes
> — Shakespeare, *Macbeth*

A tripod [of women]
stirs:

> *should we sell the beach house will*
> *the shelf fall when do I pull the plug*

while the wrens of disaster
                              flutter above
the methane cloud [the best for heat-trapping]
or CO_2 or _____

and the stage revolves
            its nothingness   belching   [blanks]

They stir the pot
They lift up their skirts   [the smell]

I predict   say all of them
The play begins   the ocean rises
                    every drop a sop or is it v.v. –
pendulous liquid poised
to
            ferry us down the drain?

The willow [weeping] breaks the well's walls
The hyacinth chokes the river
The ocean beats time

Three women dance to what they hear:
We're right
                    toes hitting ether

chance but a chain
of electrons vibrating
[almost
endlessly]   only error shitting life

Three fates   [so few]

         "Weird" means "fate"
[solarity mother]   [lunacy daughter]   [dark crone]

The lot of mortals:
Wouldn't you like to know?

The Cast

The old comedienne moves her mouth, she does her stretches, her deadpan-without-so-much-as-a-twitch, and she times it. [It's all about timing]. Old means she's timed a lot [she may have timed out]. She always wakes early with perfectly useable patter that doesn't have a story behind it. An existential joke, *tailless* they call it in the business.

The old comedienne doesn't drink her tea, her wiring's following the patter with her mouth [but not aloud]. She's slinking in a doorway when the joke comes to her, she's ready to deliver, she looks into the street and waves

to a man whose arm is in a cast, visible only at the cuff line and the stiff way he holds his arm across his chest. Why did the man cross the street, she calls out.

He veers. I'm an old comedienne, she says. Stand-up never paid.

He pats her on the head [this is not condescending, given that it's the hand sticking out of the cast, and he's very tall]. I'm walking into a bar, he says.

She doesn't even know how to make coffee, let alone a martini, which he thinks is another joke until she offers him tea.

[Offer him me? she's thinking]. The cast, after the coat is off, has no signa-tures on it – maybe he has no friends? No love life at all?

He sits on her pull-out bed. [If she kept a doily to reinforce its couch-like appearance, no one would know it pulled out at all]. She tells a tailless joke. There was a Jewish pope, she starts. You're not Jewish? she says. That's part of the patter. Nobody ever admits to being Jewish, they want to hear the joke. [She straightens her skirt].

[The man is already smiling]. He guesses the punch line and opens his palm in a ha-ha way, the palm that sticks out of the end of the cast. My arm, he says, and shakes it while he describes flying through the air after being shot out of a cannon. You know the phrase *cannon fodder?*

He forgets how it happened, paying somebody sixty dollars to stuff him into this cannon – him, the claustrophobic, the too-many-margaritas and the cash already bet. He says he can show her the burns but he would have to take off his clothes.

She sighs. [Always the competition]. Sex and death are my two best subjects, she says. She tells him with death you can do it alone and nobody laughs at you.

He saucers his cup. He's a man of the street and its crossing, he's a chrysalis and inside the cast is a new man.

[Then he's late].

As he makes his way out, he thinks of chickens, not having laid her. She [in the existential tailless way of daily life] works out another joke, this one about time, the least funny subject.

SCATTER FORCE TWO

We're two girls and we're left
                    and we're right
and fools
        for pink we walk into walls not
bars our breasts cushions vs. violent

                    bruises pink flesh
is our color not dark because
we don't walk
into doors not ours
            and no one says *Cut here*
                    our breasts

[still four] then
                    one girl leaves a pink
fool in a bar and holds her breath
so long she thinks the air's
                    going blue and scared

thus abreast we walk and walk off
                    pink bruises
the walls-not-bars in the way
            [not guys]
            the same cushions walking

pink
girls on the right and the left
                    bars imprinted
on each breast

instead of whambang
love
        [all walked out] so short
none abreast
                    none against us

BAD BOY

You know the insects' nervous-
ness, the dog attacking itself,
the tongue fritzed after a kiss.

He could've said something normal.
He could've crept into bed.
He could've flown away instead.

There's rage in average,
the sound of speed in speed.
Haste halves itself.

Your elbows crook as if to dance.
Your plants pull back at his very glance.
Your fingers ache to give him a chance.

Out of Ringing Ears

Renegade automated car says it can get us back
[Automated voice: *get us back*]

Where?

Slip of paper crushed
still warm
thigh-curved from its slept-upon
says

Called forth ring ring no sympathy
the better the sooner *get back*

Whose renegade scalp do you see taken
in a world of *get back?*

The tonic someone *(No, we have not met)*
Invisible people on stage
Clothes on hangers
[the automated voice: *get back*]

Well-dressed vs. ill-dressed she said
and *not this time* beat time

[schottische] slow polka to you

and over the table, the bedspread
                    under which a house hides
the chair-rung entrance

I wore her clothes all my life even now her blouse curses me from the closet

Pretend! Limp possum at the vet's

The chorus needs feeding
The chorus on its hind legs
The chorus breaking the toilet
The chorus, its back to Greece

Water deliciously advances
voices over it [stage mis-direction] under it
A canon signals The End

Ring, ring: [automated voice]

LIPSTICKED

A circle of lipstick on a straw

My mother's on coffee cups

The erotic crawling out, caffeinated   A skein of scenes
I'm allergic to

       Pink-colored [not-flesh] longing

chases itself

Lips across a face in a diner
Coffee cups in tiers
                 [not-hers]

You wonder: isn't poison perfect

       But are you meaning it or are you
       wanting another glass

THE DOG WITH GLASSES

The dog with glasses on her muzzle that make her look tired – Well, she says, if it isn't old so & so, chewing on my bones – the dog-faced dog, the dog that got away with everything, the dog who turns her head away [just like my mother].

VERONA NOT VENICE

The gondolas quit the shoreline for the mall
while someone insists gondola's a Greek word,
and not to sob. *Wherefore art thou?* is Shakespeare's

response: a woman at a window puts out.
We know, says all that dangerous dank water that the crowd starts
wringing. The gondolas quit the shoreline because

it's nasty: that's not gold reflecting the blue.
Be sad, sing those so many women in the mall.
Not one of them part-harmonizes, nor quotes anyone in Greek.

The shoreline is being shovelled and sold, the ur-shoreline
consists of well-proportioned houses with vertical emphasis.
If you sold one on spec, the buyer would find fault

with the continued presence of poles branded by gondoliers.
The water stays still anyway, the way heaven's must be.
Wherefore art thou? sobs the woman, a spectacle.

We might purchase gondolas two-for-one next year.
Suicides dip their toes into the water. A woman shovels
sand so you can see her proportions. *Verona!* she shouts.

SHAME HELPS

[A sudden not-breeze fills the air.]
Two men dressed in corduroy approach, one pulling a boat.
A boat of agony.
Heigh-ho. [Greeting]. [Greeting].
Fleeting smile, both. The word *smile* left on faces [of the Fourth Wall].

How to read that?
[The optic nerve gets it up].
What has been done weighs the *Heigh*.
The smarter of the men has a dollar hanging from a pocket.
Acquisitive or careless?

Balance implies a man out of sight removing his shoes.
[Why a man is the question].
The philosopher in the second row wants to punch the usher.
Such restraint stupefies the audience into paradoxical sleep:
they stop worrying but their eyeballs still roll.

And if the heavens help [with a hole in the roof] above the lights: drip, drip,
the two men look to the exit, shamed, unwilling to follow one or the other
without a speech.
Let us bury Caesar.
I hope we find some sand.
Creepy, the way birds [in stillness] sing.

GROUNDLINGS

> Capable of nothing but inexplicable dumbshows and noise
> – *Hamlet,* 3,2

One penny: the pit.
Too poor to sit.

The actor [five feet up]
sees only a sea

with small mouths gaping
[bottom feeders].

On hot days: penny-stinkers,
misbehavers.

These are the youths that thunder at a playhouse, and fight for bitten apples –
Henry VIII

Tanners, butchers, iron-workers, millers, seamen from the ships docked in the
Thames, glovers, servants, shopkeepers, wig-makers, bakers –

they waste fruit
and chestnuts [old

chestnuts] pelting
the lesser performers.

Such heaving and shoving, such itching and shouldering to sit by the women
… such toying, such smiling, such winking

Jonson despised,
and the [raucous] applause after sword fights

and theirs,
their gambling,

their wenches
calling out for a tumble.

Three hours.
The [long long] speeches.

Five hundred

well-armed groundlings
apt to quote loudly

[from other plays].

Aubade///Nocturne: To Our Ears

A woman and a man [to our ears anti-mellifluous
        but not ranting, just
noting] go into the sunrise bolted
one to the other
          by hands.

      Waves of light breakfast glamorously
with English spelling,
a woman
peeling hair from her face,
waves turning [away] wet, lapping
                            lapis [humid],
        a shore where hair sticks blue.

He, with the pronoun tucked
        into his pants, foots it,
               feet wet,
          the sun already too much. [Exeunt gulls.]
          (Do they think
of the bird without food
for days,
           the last lift-off its last,
      the gull's flap flap flap fall?)

            Caught and cold,
she is worn by him as much
as a tread on a stair,
           hard for her
on every rise.
        The darkness still nil [as nihilistic as
      youth] as if the day
were done already,
      like steak.

USAIB TITLE IX REPORT

for "Catalina Ouyang

The Panel did not believe
Complainant
slap
Respondent
are you listening?

[trigger warning]

I read it
gray-area-of-consent
here's one
        early morning

"Personal and Confidential"
engaging in
a history   in control
able to consent –
    who was awake?

Consensual is

she wrote
[trigger warning]
[trigger warning]

agrees agrees agrees
well-spoken/skilled
very clear   espouses
[trigger warning]

does not believe –

(who?) Offense Number 5

in the days and weeks
that followed
"No" presumed

demonstrated in the video

ultimately lost
"Conclusions" and "Findings"
threw keys   [gyrated]
          and stood
was an erratic

rescind the   No
[trigger warning]
expressed

no physical
          both explained at
her capacities and able
[accordingly violation]
            was in control

please see the [attached
detailed] accounts

WHAT? IS YOUR LINE

I think I'm panicking
I think I'm panicking
etc.
crying practice

[windowless]

quick, a dream:
one of you accuses the other

What? is your line
the gun is fake but you need a license

Miss Vulgarity comes forward in
a lack-of-bathing-suit competition

a different voice speaking "I"
to an "audience"

and rants: *and you and you and you*
and *it wasn't like that*

brief interview with an innocent bystander
before the lover slash narrator finds his way over

floating along and then the queen says
women were at best queens then

WE

the chorus   too loud
but that is opinion
      answers back: even the building is burning

[insert choreography]
where who keeps the extinguisher where backstage

THE SCOTTISH PLAY

a soliloquy piped in over the vacant stage
[b.g. sound: ice cubes]   [coffee pouring]

someone says words and then you see "tomorrow" and "tomorrow" and "to-
morrow"rephrase on the LCD at lights out: "the instruments of darkness
tell truths"

arch language [better algorithms]
moveable elements: not chairs but guilt: Duncan's guilty Malcolm's guilty the
omniscient writer's guilty   two drunk chamberlains

walk forward and fear that the forest is walking forward
[involuntary shriek]

speak as if to camera although it's a play
switch locations: Banquo in the bathroom   Macduff behind his computer in
Maryland

all scenes contained in this poem   *What Luck!*

two chairs face the audience   the first chair coughs   an explosion of daggers
here is the garden   she points to the sink   *here is the castle and points to the
air vent*

characters walk in from another scene   IT SAVES MONEY
names but no dialogue [they all stand there silent then sleepwalk]

Silverware Dialogue

A fork and a spoon lie together
to spoon and to fork.

$E = MC^2$ says the spoon.
I don't have the energy says the fork.

Forgiveness? says the spoon.
It is as if we lie on a vast table

says the fork. Useless.
The spoon measures a dose.

Sink to your knees. The fork
submits. [The past is prescient.]

The spoon clasps the fork.
Of course, says the spoon,

it's all about portion control.
Let's sleep says the fork.

Weep? the spoon says.
The spoon is sorry too, like the song.

Make me toast says the fork, and snappy.
The spoon says, Who turned on

the lights? Birds begin singing
their favorite: *O moon, O moon.*

The table was laid, says the spoon,
not me. Tines, my dear, are everything,

says the fork. My tines are retired.
They spoon through course

after intercourse, the hunger being
incurable, inconsolable.

Emma's Play

[Characters gather round a coffin to act out a piece of history, in this case Emma Goldman's.]

THIRD LOVER: You see that Red Scare on her? The way she never smiled. Not even the undertaker could twist her lips.

FIRST LOVER: Not the Red Scar?

SECOND LOVER: I'm her favorite lover. We were in a four way. I was second. It was free love.

THIRD LOVER: Free? I went to prison. I tried to kill a capitalist and became sympathetic to gay men inside. Maybe too sympathetic. Jack London wouldn't front my book. I was her first lover.

FIRST LOVER: Take a number.

EMMA'S CORPSE: None of you is the guy I married. He was Josef. I married him twice. The FBI didn't think that was enough, and deported me.

FOURTH LOVER: I was paid. [She flashes her thigh].

THIRD LOVER: That's out of character. You flashed your thigh for free.

FOURTH LOVER: So what? It's a free country.

Force is at the door [clarion]. [A voice command, a voice prompt]: Open the door.

[Everyone goes sober not getting the door].

FOURTH LOVER: I'm an alien. Like, not a citizen, all right? Like illegal. Like an immigrant. That's why I can't get a real job, one with taxes and withholding and obligations to the system, that's why I have to get paid, and in cash.

All but the FOURTH LOVER laugh. [The door remains unopened while they take up a collection].

THIRD LOVER: How cold is Emma's corpse? It's been practically a century. She would never tell you she was cold, she fought deportation as well as personal detail. What did she have to do with the Palmer Raids? Half of those bombs were planted by J. Edgar Hoover in his own backyard.

EMMA'S CORPSE: Who remembers Hoover? [Picks up the corded phone].

SECOND LOVER: Emma always gets the last word. *Ta,* she would say, if nothing else.

FIRST LOVER: Breath through the lungs, *ta* expelled when the undertaker undertook this job.

SECOND LOVER: You're the hairy writer Emma thought Ben would like, the capitalist-killer?

[THIRD LOVER nods]

FIRST LOVER: You have no choice but to accept me now, Emma.

SECOND LOVER: I want to do something original, for once. Not the party line. [Prying First Lover off Emma's Corpse].

THIRD LOVER: It is what it is.

EMMA'S CORPSE: Skip the tautology. [Untangles phone cord, hangs up without an answer].

FOURTH LOVER: Something, something, something. In a bag.

[Bag hangs in mid-air, over the corpse, with a zipper up one side, an unfailing zipper as yet unzipped for the million future dead unfree to come, despite Emma's love and ambition, for the free-for-all].

Let Freedom Ring

In the Every Day we set
our faces
                              draw eyebrows
          cock our heads in disguise

          Would we recognize freedom amongst us
if he peeled
          the pantyhose off his face?
if he romped through the waving grain?

Thus disoriented, looking for the bell clapper

the cue coming up fast, the play
relentless, in this regard always half-assed

          [what kind of ass is that?]
          its confines a quarter turn tighter
like a mental illness undiagnosed,

                    we bell-ring
                    O it's Friday
                              that kind of freedom
or act as ringers
for a celebrity you wouldn't know what to say to after all this anyway

                    Come on –
don't fright, no bolting, even if what you hear
                    so soon loud is
          confusing
                    The *to be* verb
cancels the simulacrum

                    to be or not
               is real, the theater is
only patriots

32

their uniforms
their regiment
unless they enforce
otherwise

SPECTACLE

Not only Disney Hall lit [42 projectors] in the land of glitz,
but a lone woman making a spectacle of herself before

11 Congressmen [not Congresspeople] who imagine themselves
with her and the clothing removal part, or at least peeking in.

Loud music over those projectors, and the German goose step,
the atomic bomb of post-civility, the plane headed into the building,

thrice-told lies while millions watch [believing everything they hear].
As the face of spectacle, whom do the gladiators mesmerize?

Spectators [the root of spectacle] grin in their awe, in their sin
of dissolving, one into the other, into a ripple of *Yes, I'm less.*

Malaprops

> To illiterate him, I say, quite from your memory
> – Mrs. Malaprop in *The Rivals*

What props come slaved to the tape marks?
Mrs. Mal, the evil elusive and-of-course-essential
cigar box containing the gun for the table,
has a meltdown in the green room
and no one finds her in time.

From behind his lapel, the actor fingershoots
the opposition who fake-falls to the sound cue.
Mrs. Mal chuckles into the base of the curtain
where deposited, smoking the last cigar of the box.
Whoo-ha, her chuckle catches fire

and the applause burns down the house.
Mrs. Mal asks for a bigger credit.
The tape marks where she should sit
curl and go vague. In Philadelphia
the gun takes up a collection

to retire Mrs. Mal to singing backstage.
She moans. Other props do not sympathize,
their grime and every day grim
fray like nerves in a skull. They
lose themselves in self-pity.

Mrs. Mal is boxed in. The Cuban girl
in a headdress Copacabanas her closed.
The gun finds a holster unsexed.
The stage, alert as always, lit and strewn
with effort, calls the curtain back.

No Props

Good use is put to sadness [even that] plucking
at their Adam's apples
        [Eve looks away, physiognomy
at its worst]
        and teeth gnashing
their dental scare

they switch on and off
        [lives where fish are thrown
into the darling deeps]
                Awk!

O Eve O Eve [weeps one]
            a being unbearable
        [trucks shudder at the shutters]
        Is he rehearsing?

        There's no telling

shouts one now band-aided
            [emotes with a kiss]
            Secrecy's a powerboat
[also lights]

One goof gets rent   goes gooey
in direct address
           [it takes two for applause]
     one gives

Nobody Knows How to Put Her Out

It takes five hours to perform. [Five hours go by]. He stretches his legs clear across the stage, watch! Something very boring happens again. [A fly punctuates].

A lute and a bass drum embattle. [One with a stick].

She lays a basket at his feet as big as his head. [It is his head].
A headless guy runs around on those feet. [Spasms].

She burns the bill from all the bridge crossings. [The ash floating up triggers balloons to float down].
She burns the bill again [a xerox copy]. This time she steps on the burst balloons and tracks the ash around.
He sweeps up the ash and rubs it into new balloons, crooning, *You never needed me more.*

The headless guy runs offstage. [Cast of three].

The characters bite [With a wrist-flick, the die, the solemn die, rolls] with a line of *of* description after: Margaret of Willendorf, the Venus of Margaret, the alias "John" for confusion until there's a setting [the knife too sharp, the fork with only two tines].
Of course they speak – what kind of setting is this?
The fork insists on saying there's a table under it. [The wood grain's fabulous.] The knife is annoyed by tiny flying saucers that heave off their cups as soon as they see a napkin flap.

You've got your betrayer who wears polka dots that fall off, whimsy finished, you've got your eponymous *Enter here* guy [whose line was cut] who will later cut the betrayer's line, only don't say I said so. The trees barely hold up [the canvas they're painted on] until emotional violence breaks out because that's when the audience remembers [it wants] to piss. La-la-la and it's over. Please take your seats [but not too far].

[Something strange happens].

He tells us about what's going on, human to human, over the vacuum cleaner that so musically makes its way across the stage, tells us as if you're standing behind the pulled curtain [monocle-alert] electrified.

Normal stuff: a man pulling lint off his black pants while elsewhere, the sound of a toilet backing up, a "same as before" scene, only now with [a crisis because of] the presence of a louder audience.
Someone is hit. Verbal or mental? [Pharmaceutical?]

Darkness, monotone singing, singing, singing, words you almost can remember while the room fills with whisper [a crescendo of it].
How revolutionary! murmurs the wall.
Could be the fourth. [You wish].

Reading from a diary, someone else's [while the someone else stands there] lips moving. Someone's dead in the diary and there's a knocking on the door. No, that's not what the diary says, says the script. Lips do move, reading it, just not the deads.' Only they're the only ones you want to hear. Re-hearse. [Hearse].

It's all right, Dear.

The policeman doesn't answer to Dear. [Emergency-not-emergency]. It's just sex, she says. Don't you love a uniform?

Enough, he says. Something ludicrous happens then: the policeman, exposing himself more. She laughs [and shouldn't have]. A strange man.

Next scene: same event. [Someone different standing there, taking turns standing there].

Coming to lunch? he asks.

You wouldn't believe me if I told you, she says.

The same lunch three times.

A monologue by a strange man. About a strange world. [About our strange world].

I would like very much to talk about dirt. [Pause]. [Pause]. [Pause]. But I'm a woman with my thumb stuck in the bathroom flusher.

[Muffled cries]. [My feet remain visible]. [The curtains are still open but it's the wrong day].

What's wrong with it? asks the strange man.

I know what's in the trunk of her car. It ain't love but it ain't bad. What is she doing, looking for heat? It's gonna hurt. *Is it gonna hurt?* is her question. "A Work Related Accident" is what she uses to equilibrate herself. Someone is strangling swans, that's the other sound. The dead talk [the way they do] with the accents of silence, and her head bursts into flame [or burns like a cigarette, or starts to glow]. But nobody smokes anymore so nobody knows how to put her out.

TWO

DAD OR GOD?

Air, a known substance
but invisible, then –
   See it out your mouth?
Dad laughs in the cold, a cloud
        off
his teeth.

Consider condensation – nothing, tasteless
at best,
spirit humping psyche, description:
   zero like Coke.

The dictator hung from the ceiling,
   the doves looking at his feet,
     an old lady saying
clean your wax out, cruelty's everywhere:
      only when the outside pretends
      it's different
   from the inside
is it news.

We're gripping each other,
rhythm-method, species-bound, and the earth shakes
   and spooks. It could be bad and not love,
that shake and spook.

   Catherine the Great bade dwarves to copulate on ice,
   then stay the night in her frozen
     palace. Blue
   and near dead by morning, new-balded,
they were ghostly, so cold they showed no breath
at all.

God or Dad laughs. We like
to hear this: we juggle,

read out loud,
　　　　burp –

He makes his own joke,
　　　　　　and flies arise
　　　　　　out of nowhere.

Moon Theater

On parade with the old dog doing her best,
we walk between two bodies of water,
not an island but wet blue [ribbons]

lapping land, and come upon a boy on a chair.
We do not have curbs on our lane so the chair
is where the lawn [such as sand permits]

begins, and the boy [who should be
at some screen] says *There!* and points
to what I've missed, head down with the dog:

the hot moon where our little tarmac
and the water rise up [to sink it],
suspended as if thrown and stuck

to a velcro black, its orange huge. Attending
is what the boy is doing, and the dog,
head lifted, begins his bark.

King Leer

By day and night she wrongs me.
The fool laughs as if Dad's joking.

Of course a king's esteem is inflated.
Pump the dog's stomach for Viagra,

hear Let me alone but don't leave me,
your mother is dead, you will do.

From the fool a/k/a the daughters' pov
he's plain angry: I'll sue you unto the grave.

Perhaps his trouble is vascular?
His heart, stented like a kite, his heart gone.

The judge in him knows the cost of lawyers.
Let's kill them all, he says, and hires three.

Age as narcissistic injury. Freud rages too:
he's just a child. We pay the retainers.

But what of his hundred knights, galloping off?
Dad grabs the phone. We prefer to think he was mad

from the start, we didn't bring it on, this storm in his head.
I nothing am, says Mother floating on her deathbed.

How sharper than a serpent's tooth.
Still the shrink says let him be, let his lawyers

devise more wills and break what laws he wishes.
I'll outlive prison, whole governments,

for he has a decreased need for sleep,
and is distracted by the price of corn

and corporate law, and greed. Yet he writes checks
for thousands to the caregiver, our proxy.

She'll put out or I'll sue, he says. *Let copulation thrive.*
We cook and cook and cook that he might be reached

through ribs. He gorges, and forgets he eats.
Cure old age, he demands. Forthwith,

his college sends an emissary across the state.
The estate, as they call it, is all up here.

He points to his head. He kisses the shrink.
Which of you shall we say doth love us most?

He flicks the lights on, bedroom by bedroom,
We bolt upright, glimpsing the knife.

BLANK PINK MALL

The color of pretty,
of the sink just before the rinse
            is finished, [dilute] blood.

Cheap, you say, but there it is,
            Rorschach's wall +
corner = home, a pink petticoat,

ripped, with a safety pin
pinned to skin. It's your work
            to assert the walls inside

            aren't black [and my glasses
are colored wrong]. Seep love into it,
praise the blood pumping,

the heart plump until the siphon
            slips and all rushes
[with eagerness] out.

            Pink-haired [pink-hairy]
disappears behind the door:
                  it's not a color,

it's a code, a number on the paint can
            before Hopper emptied
the premises, his wife [left inside],

bruised and weeping. [Still he thinks:
            more flat light]. The female
[like this] isn't washed clean

or even pink-washed, the girl's left
holding the dripping cord:
a mall-birthed girl.

      You thought male?
The marquee's all virgin-power,
the kind that won't talk.

The Glassine

[A VERY THIN AND SMOOTH PAPER WHICH IS AIR AND WATER RESISTANT]

Befuddled, yet amorous, the comma anticipates [pauses to consider or reconsider] the Wait-a-minute stance – but then Buddy interrupts to bark his last [unless that's a form for shoes]. I'd never walk a shod dog. I'm befuddled. Those flowers!

That's accusatory, that's not getting any closer to the amorous unless that yellow plant in your arms is for me. For or about? barks Buddy. I upload those arms, hands are involved, the very hands of love that sweat only up to arousal then, confused by their extra-ness, *which hand to take* not *where's the other one?* I drop them. Loss [or neglect] is so quick to interject.

Stupendous [the actual pause] the potential, the pre-barked moment: "I could have danced all night," the yellow plant, the flowers on their stalks not yet fruit [nor blown], the spring that dogs Buddy's energy portend that sinks into a meld of all the harbingers, the I [of this] hoped real enough. Who could find the comma to resist?

ALPHABET

Portraits of graduates line the room, even the children
of the second wife, even her! as dead as your husband.

He was taken and beaten – governor at last – at last released
but falling to the ground, your son putting a phone

to his head. You were in Egypt, in exile, safe.
All he said was A-B-C-D, what men repeat

during torture so they reveal nothing, or to bear it
without screaming, or remembering how they learned

the alphabet under a tree, with the flies thick
and the good smell of milk on their hands.

A-B-C-D, you say over tea. Have a biscuit?
I helped you cook long ago, cross-legged on cement

in a soot black kitchen open to the sky.
In the yard, a circle of chairs,

your husband pouring the scotch
of some aid worker wanting some permission.

When kerosene half-lit their faces, the speeches began.
Ret tried to hush them, but they went on and on

into the absolute black of the Sudanese night,
democracy off-stage, just a little beyond.

EMERGENCY EXIT

[Gets more attention than the lead after being replaced by an understudy
who isn't as needy].

The EXIT minds its own business, loitering really, in its red suit,
waiting for patrons to scream

about smoke and the entitlement of season ticket holders who have
easier access to exits. The usher

stationed beneath it, greets latecomers in sign language, a scolding motion.
But when the front row regular

exits mid-soliloquy, no alarm sounds except from the director
who's preparing his notes [transparent lies].

USHER

Torn down in 1830, the Usher House hid two bodies embracing in its cellar. [Now a three-block area in modern Boston].

POE: Mr. and Mrs. Luke Usher, the friends and fellow actors of my mother who took care of me while she died.

DEBUSSY: I died, writing the Poe opera. [Colon cancer].

Madness, resurrection, the living twin of the buried girl, plus *opium, opium, opium*: a knell.

NOT TO MENTION: An usher as doorkeeper for when you have a palace, or the Palace Theater.

Eye-like windows in the Poe flat, fissure in the Poe masonry the usher points at: your seat.

NOT TO MENTION: He doesn't escort you out.

An Audio Tour of Helen Jewett's Murder in Downtown New York City

Stand outside the Con Ed building. Have you ever wondered about this monolith? It's like the past, lips sealed, no entry – a murder site.

No one hears her scream. In 1836 the brownstone's walls were double thick, one building flush against another. Like the past.

Long convoluted speeches and ridiculous clothes in the past, not to mention habits. Writing letters three times a day saying things like:

curlicue curlicue curlicue

The murder wasn't supposed to happen, it was no mob job. She was a prostitute. Rather famous in her time, even the mayor knew who she was.

Ahem.

As in all crime stories, the past represents the dark and sensitive, and links up to the present, that is to say, the dead living, O.J. for example, so when you feel the breath of the assassin on your, I mean her, neck, you empathize.

Think dominance. Turn around. Look again.

The city detectives moved into this building fifty years after her murder. They let journalists investigate, publish all the details, even solve the murder. Or, in her case, deflect the guilt.

Walk along Wall Street where the post office operates beside a dog park.

Helen parades daily to the post office in the best finery-as-advertisement she can afford. She learned penmanship and good graces while a serving maid in upstate New York. You know those gigantic houses along the river, or even just the ones with five bedrooms? They housed servants dying to get out of there. If not actual death, getting out usually meant factory work. Not for Helen. After De Tocqueville, one of the many European travel writers casting judgment on the American savages, knocks on her employers' door and writes that she was most impressive, she uses guile and sex to rework fate.

The family lets her go. Not sad or embarrassed, she has her bag packed.

Consider the business, the risks she has to take. Money is everywhere then too.

And horses, noisy with clipclop, vendors shrieking. She likes to eat oysters from carts, a junk food then and you'd be lucky if you didn't get a bad one. She flirts.

He strolls the streets, overdressed as males always seemed to be then, spats, tails, and a cape. He takes off, running to work on Broadway along with hundreds of other nineteen-year-old youths. Youths, the sound of the word thick and ancient.

Imagine an alley. Once fenced. Her place.

Private watchmen, three of them, posted near the corner. Her madam runs out into the night. She's dead, she screams. Somebody goes flying by, carrying a bloody hatchet, leaps over the fence, and runs down the alley. A cape tassel catches on a picket.

Evidence. The detectives have it.

Her bedroom is upstairs, so quiet with its double-thick walls. The watchmen cough on smoke, climbing the stairs. The body is charred, a botched job by an amateur – it's hard to get a body to burn – the skull's crushed by a hatchet, letters strewn everywhere.

Did she say no to his demand for money? The drawer still contained a small sum. Or was it really about love, that fury?

Feel yourself moving freely down the street, in the present, alive. Stop at the courthouse, all those steps.

The accused took to wearing a kind of beret that became all the fashion. A thousand men his age paraded around town wearing them. They showed up at the trial, waving the berets, and the newspaper with its story.

There's a newspaper stand on your right.

He spoke while being held in prison before the trial, a first for the newspapers, which had never used interviews before, and he was very cocky.

It's unfathomable that he could be guilty.

Your cellphone rings. A quiet voice on the other end tells you not to turn around. Very convincing.

CHAIR THEATER

A cardboard proscenium
and two players: a chair

and a tree, together only
in the context of Xmas.

There should be a rug,
music, an entrance.

Instead, internal anguish,
external stasis, limited

animation, a voice off-stage,
singing about silence and night.

Premise: they are both wood.
Which burns first?

The tree breaks the chair,
sitting on it.

Patience is coiled in the rungs.
Another needle falls.

DXM as Bond

[cough, cough]

A sideways stride-crouch
toward your husband, *je suis
fatigué!* the cell threatening,
[not a Commie's],
your husband with his hands up
and soaped, the syrup
of cell death sliding
off, the cell-laden wind lifting
the lace of my old lady
armchair, once dressed
in a bikini [my torso]
because this

is crossfire: the bullets bouncing
like mercury loosed from its
sheath, sex leftover from
the last scene barely remembered
as lived, the bikini straps
broken, you as unfaithful
as the butler that exits with
his hesitation intact, almost
thoughtful, swaying away,
feverish fevered the tense past.
The bodies pile up.

On our knees now for
Deus X. Machina to drop
his big hypodermic
from the cloud [not the place
that remembers every keystroke].
Hear DXM complain:
Always with the sky.
Scanning it, nonetheless,

for Bond tailoring, we wait
in uxorial non-hand-holding,
getting old, getting older,
antibodies still very pro.

Dark Daddy

The dark daddy went about the hushed place in a turncoat. You can suspender him, said the allegory, the one moralizing that such a dad wasn't Good-For-The-Planet, that such a dad had better watch his feet in said place. The place pivoted and the dark daddy went down. Are there flames? Is there fissure? Barked – instead of said – the alligator. For that, a chorus strode in, in tailless interjection. Halleluia, they chorused, hoarse the way the word makes you, and loud. Nobody heard what the dark daddy said as he bent even lower to do what? Bent? You bet he's bent, said the allegator, alleging more. The hushiness of the place shrugged off their silence – the chorus, the allegory, the dark daddy symbolized in clamor. The rasp of metal, the screech of chalk, the *of of of.* The place pivoted again, nobody could hold it, the alligator and the chorus keeping their footing by dropping to all fours, a technique all instinct. The dark daddy never got himself closed over, he just went darker, bent over. Where are the chains we ordered? the chorus raved in ascending arpeggios. The allegator alleged: He left his coat. Together they rent it in two until all that was left was the hush.

Backstage: Fear Ducts

Animal urges first.

Then the Unconscious talks:
a demon, a daimon
                            insistent on the spectacle,
yes, an a.m. celebration but already

a tinge bruised, spats too tight.

The animal
midday

says she feels faint.

You say *raggy?* There she is,
at the feet of
                            Unconscious
who flits off, the noble toga slipping.
Hello?

                An MRI emerges
with its wicked racket. Yet

espresso at dusk goes down
as elixir. [Performance, okay?]

                The animal mirror
suggests it's you on the back, silvered
to hold all fear

                and that some of that
will still
sing, the mouth
        opened in terror.

She Said He Said

What she couldn't say
he didn't say.

The boy hit the cement, he said.
What she said the dog barked over.

But he didn't say that.
She didn't say, she didn't say.
Not arguing.

The eyes of the dog so full and clear
said it all.

In a critical state, she said. ICU, she said.
He said, I'm sorry.
So sorry meant something else.

The long snaky line from neuron to tongue through the crush of synapse, a
pod of mitochondria, even the flavor of old chocolate in the wet surround of
mouth. Until she, taking her tongue in hand, as it were, said.

An envelope of silence. Licked shut.

No one said a thing. The boy,

he said later. Later it was said
she said a series of unkindnesses.
Why? he said.

There the boy lies, crumpled, on the cement.
The wind came up and no one could hear what she said but she said it for
forty years. As if smoothed.

For there we were: he said, she said, in hetero forever do us part.
Whispered so she could hear other saids in all the vowels heretofore because.

Her mouth is Munch-open.
No one is hearing that? he said.

The boy landed on the cement.

No one actually said that.
No one said *the boy*.
They used his name, the one on the tag and in the paper
she said, though not often.

The boy will die and so will I, he said.

And the crow, she said, and the squirrel with his pitted acorn, the fish lithe in
water, the lizard perched on the crack, even and most especially the attractive
blue heron, feathers ruffled by what, she said, unable to fly today and even
less so tomorrow, standing on the bank as if at theater.

He said a cascade of Not-To-Be-Forgottens, and she said the rest. And if she
didn't say it, she would have.

The boy did die the way they do, on cement.
What? she said. What?

As it has been said: the boy flew away on a blue chariot.
The reverse of cement: air and interstices where, she said, one could.

He said she said.

Writer Doesn't Mention the Trap Door

FIRST ACTOR: Turn up the kliegs!

SECOND ACTOR: Don't call me actress. Beatrice is good. You called the last one Penelope. Penny in the plea-bargain scene. Cheap.

FIRST ACTOR: Look, if someone's looking for me, are they going to yell *First Actor?* Ben is better. But better if we don't alliterate. Beatrice, Ben? No gravitas, no gravy.

BEATRICE: But it's Dantesque: lost in the woods because of me. Not the plea bargain. On second thought, call me Ishmael. Or even Cheryl.

BEN: The waves plunge us deeper. Hang on!

BEATRICE: Ham, it has to be ham. That's a nice Biblical name.

BEN: Impugning me? Or – actor eats a ham sandwich before the plea-bargain? Remember, I'm observant, vegan, low salt, no gluten.

BEATRICE: Stick to the script. Literally, like, duct tape. I have a babysitter and she goes home in an hour.

BEN: Lost in space. I can do that.

BEATRICE: The bassinet in the living room, the sadness and anger of maternity, not to mention the trap door.

BEN: Oops.

BEATRICE: Only four more lines. Nobody liked Ben anyway.

WRITER: *She follows him everywhere.*

VISCERA

Like blueberries,

the rubbed-white chalk sheen crushed,
and the sky's two tone at dusk across a face

bruise-beautiful [myself inside out].

A shovel would work, long-handled
in the big silence of the gray pool I stand in,
[lipsticked air, a kissing woman].

There's the rusty smell of red, the package from inside myself
        so well designed the label is hidden

[and worn backward].
Think of the self strewn, a constellation hunched,

a shadow so dark it can't be seen.

The language of fruit tears my throat:
smashed petals, fruit rotting in process, [the green] one

red.

Fortunate are those who look where they step,
see the stain go on.

SCHIPPERKES

Groan ellipsis groan,
sand on sheets, canalboat

noir.

Who gives this dog the what for?

Schipperkes ran messages for the Resistance on the rivers,
Hello stuck in the bullet, a 4-legged cancan effort.

There's a song in that very dog,

there's Cointelpro:

a series of covert and, at times,
illegal projects conducted by the FBI aimed at
surveilling, infiltrating, discrediting,
and disrupting domestic political organizations
which only perhaps ended in 1971.

> Aeschylus, dad of tragedy and 75 lost plays
whose Cassandra foretells the murder of Agamemnon,
enters the palace.

Bark. Bark.

HOUSE OF ATRIUM

I.

Heart – check. Receives blood, forces it
forward. Dance to it [Cue glitter ball].

Skylit also, many storied, like a whole book.
Atria's cousins in short-shorts,

in candy-color. See the above great-
great whip out of the shadows:

the mother taken by the brother,
some soccer-headed Greeks

harming the hood, doors
banging, gangbanging, house

or whore, the one who ends up
rich. At. Least. Binge. [Bear appears.]

II.

The hotels had it: a 70's architecture
where fathers in y-fronts dance,

locked out. Couture-bound,
these people, soft, lacy,

the No-Parking-after-8-kind
complement the atrium

with capitals and $$$. Watch, the little Atria
spend-and-thrifts. The heat of day pours

through, with requisite light, a Rome,
a coliseum humming with volunteers

from other royal houses. A lion, or no lion?
Black-tipped or tailed?

III.

The breeze Greeks the house, a Vesuvius
tells all. But there's the whole afternoon,

a dog who guards what's mortgaged,
sublet up the kazoo. [Who has a key?]

The subdivision condemns
what it can. Two men force

their way in, amulet-heavy. Nobody
prefers to be sacrificed: a prince

disguised as a shepherd,
the dog about to give the plot away.

But wait, an Atria calls,
no one is sick yet.
[Exeunt, pursued by Bear].

ABOUT THE AUTHOR

TERESE SVOBODA is the author of *Professor Harriman's Steam Air-Ship, When the Next Big War Blows Down the Valley: Selected and New Poems, All Aberration, Laughing Africa, Treason, Mere Mortals, Weapons Grade,* and the chapbook, *Dogs Are Not Cats. Treason* was republished in 2020 by Double-back Books.

A recent Guggenheim recipient, Svoboda has won the Iowa Prize in Poetry, the Cecil Hemley Award and the Emily Dickinson Prize from the Poetry Society of America, and a New York Foundation for the Arts grant in poetry. An NEH fellow in translation, she also received a PEN/Columbia fellowship to translate Nuer song. She has taught at Williams, Columbia's School of the Arts, Southampton/Stony Brook, the New School, San Francisco State, William and Mary, Fairleigh Dickinson, Sarah Lawrence, Bennington, the Atlantic Center for the Arts, the Universities of Tampa, Miami, and Hawaii, Fordham, and Wichita State, in St. Petersburg, Tblisi, and Kenya for the Summer Literary Program, and has held the McGee Chair at Davidson College. She is also the author of seven books of fiction, a memoir, a book of translation from the Nuer, and a biography of the radical poet Lola Ridge.